W9-BXW-274

Bone Detectives

by Gretchen McBride

PEARSON

Scott
Foresman

Editorial Offices: Glenview, Illinois • Parsippany, New Jersey • New York, New York
Sales Offices: Needham, Massachusetts • Duluth, Georgia • Glenview, Illinois
Coppell, Texas • Ontario, California • Mesa, Arizona

Every effort has been made to secure permission and provide appropriate credit for photographic material. The publisher deeply regrets any omission and pledges to correct errors called to its attention in subsequent editions.

Unless otherwise acknowledged, all photographs are the property of Scott Foresman, a division of Pearson Education.

Photo locators denoted as follows: Top (T), Center (C), Bottom (B), Left (L), Right (R), Background (Bkgd)

Opener: ©DK Images, Corbis; 1 ©DK Images; 3 ©DK Images; 4 ©DK Images; 5 ©DK Images; 6 ©DK Images; 7 Corbis; 8 Robert Harding World Imagery; 9 Corbis; 10 ©DK Images; 11 ©DK Images; 12 Photo Researchers, Inc.; 14 ©DK Images; 16 Corbis; 17 ©DK Images; 19 Corbis

ISBN: 0-328-13610-7

Copyright © Pearson Education, Inc.

All Rights Reserved. Printed in the United States of America. This publication is protected by Copyright, and permission should be obtained from the publisher prior to any prohibited reproduction, storage in a retrieval system, or transmission in any form by any means, electronic, mechanical, photocopying, recording, or likewise. For information regarding permission(s), write to: Permissions Department, Scott Foresman, 1900 East Lake Avenue, Glenview, Illinois 60025.

6 7 8 9 10 V0G1 14 13 12 11 10 09 08 07

PALEONTOLOGY

What is paleontology?

The word *paleontology* comes from the Greek language. The first half of the word means "old" or "ancient." The second half of the word means "branch of learning." Paleontology is the study of the forms of life that existed in prehistoric times. Paleontologists are scientists who study fossils, or the remains or traces of the animals and plants that lived millions of years ago. They uncover evidence of ancient life by digging in different places on Earth. They study their finds in laboratories. They develop theories, or explanations, about what the Earth was like in the time before recorded history.

This is a fossil of a *Psittacosaurus* showing most of the skeleton with the skull, neck, and spinal column prominent.

Paleontology didn't really exist as a science until the early 1800s. However, for hundreds of years, people had collected odd stones that looked like parts of large bones. They wanted to know where they came from. They also wondered about the shells of sea creatures they found far from the sea.

Many collectors realized that these fossils were from animals that no longer existed. Some related their finds to legends. Then in the 1800s people began to realize that the stones were fossils—the remains of extinct animals. Read on to learn about the work of some of these pioneers, and then find out what today's paleontologists do.

Paleontologists and workmen in the 1800s excavated dinosaur bones on the side of a rocky cliff in Sussex, England.

Leonardo da Vinci
(1452–1519)

This great artist and inventor collected and studied fossils.

An ammonite fossil

Vanished Oceans and Dragon's Teeth

As long ago as 500 B.C., ancient Greek philosophers found fossils. They recognized the curious things they found as traces of living things. When they found seashells far from the sea, the Greeks realized that an ocean must have once covered the land that they were standing on.

For many centuries Chinese people collected fossils and ground them into powder to use in medicines. They called the large teeth they found "dragon's teeth." They thought that these giant teeth might have come from the dragons they heard about in stories.

Pioneers of Paleontology

Robert Plot (1640–1696) was a naturalist, or someone who studies nature. He was also an historian working in England in the 1600s. He found a fossilized bone and knew that it had come from a creature that once lived in the area. The piece of bone he found measured almost two feet around and weighed twenty pounds! Plot realized that a creature with a bone this large would have been enormous.

At first, Plot thought that the bone came from an elephant brought to Britain by the Romans. Then he decided that the bone must have belonged to a giant human! His find became part of the collection at the Ashmolean Museum in Oxford, England.

Robert Plot thought he had discovered the fossil of a legendary creature. Of course, this was not the case. It would be many years before a paleontologist would examine Plot's fossil and identify his find as a bone from a very large dinosaur called *Megalosaurus.*

The Ashmolean Museum, England's first museum, is open to the public.

The fossil-bearing Lias beds on Monmouth
Beach, Lyme Regis, England

She Sells Seashells

As a child, Mary Anning walked the beaches of Lyme
Regis in the south of England. She was collecting fossils.
Mary's father was a carpenter, but the family found it
hard to make ends meet. So they sold the fossils they
found to tourists for extra money.

Mary's father taught her how to find fossils in the
treacherous stone cliffs of Lyme Regis. She kept finding
and selling fossils after he died when she was eleven.

The tourists who bought the fossils believed they were
"snake stones" to be used as a protection. Mary Anning
knew that the fossils held a far more interesting secret.

Her older brother Joseph sometimes assisted Mary in her beachcombing. One day Joseph noticed a strange shape under the sand. He uncovered a huge skull. Its enormous, bony eye sockets were staring back at him from the sand. When he later tried to show Mary where he had made his discovery, he found that a mud slide had covered the area.

A year later, when Mary was twelve years old, she uncovered the complete skeleton. It was seventeen feet long. It would later be identified as an ichthyosaur. Then, in 1823, Mary Anning brought to light the bones of another unknown creature. It was a hit in the scientific community. The creature was named *Plesiosaurus*.

A fossilized ichthyosaur skeleton

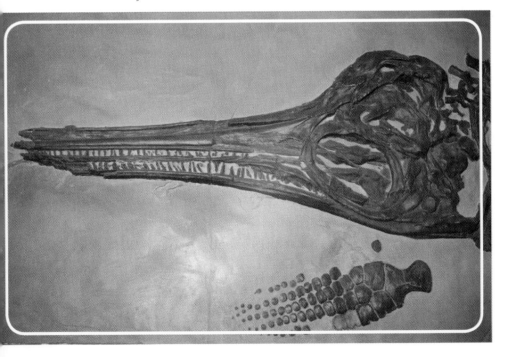

The Scholar with a Pet Bear

William Buckland (1784–1856) of Oxford University was a serious geology scholar. Geology is the study of the earth. He was also an animal enthusiast. Buckland filled his house with creatures, including guinea pigs, a jackal, and his party-loving pet bear.

Buckland respected the work of Mary Anning and joined her in searching for specimens when he visited Lyme Regis. Buckland lent his support to Anning and others interested in the growing field of fossil study. Later he would make significant contributions of his own.

Around 1815 Buckland found several bones of a large beast. He examined the teeth, jaws, and limb bones. He concluded that they had come from some kind of extinct lizard. He named the creature *Megalosaurus*. However, he noted that the teeth were not attached to the jaw the way the teeth of living lizard species were. This creature's teeth were set into sockets in the jaw. Buckland himself would not recognize the importance of this distinction. A few years later, Sir Richard Owen would.

These bones would be the first fossils recognized as the remains of a huge extinct reptile—a dinosaur.

These teeth and pieces of jawbone led Buckland to conclude that giant lizards once existed. *Megalosaurus* was the first dinosaur to be named—several years before the word dinosaur existed!

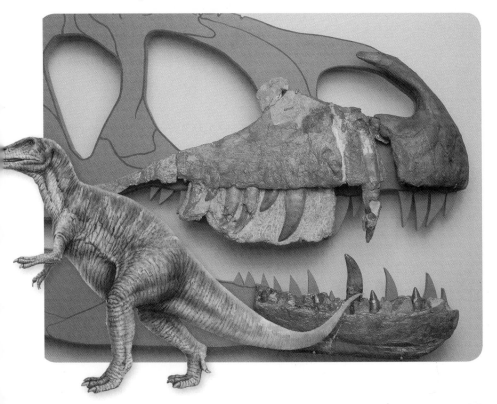

The Father of Paleontology

Even after these discoveries, paleontology was still not considered a scientific discipline, or a field with established rules and standards to govern the work. Baron Georges Cuvier of Paris is now credited with bringing the collection and study of fossils to the level of a science.

Baron Cuvier was an expert in comparative anatomy, which is the study of how the parts of one animal compare to similar parts of other animals. He applied the rules of anatomy to his work when he analyzed fossils. He was able to make educated guesses about the appearance of the animal the fossil had come from.

Baron Georges Cuvier
(1769–1832)

Baron Cuvier realized that the huge animals he was identifying were not roaming a still unexplored part of the world but must be extinct.

One of Owen's Crystal Palace dinosaur models

A New Word

Like Cuvier, Richard Owen (1804–1892) was an expert in comparative anatomy. His knowledge led him to realize that some of the enormous beasts that left bones behind were not simply large lizards. Their legs did not attach to their bodies the way a lizard's legs do. They also were not like any modern reptiles. Owen called this new group of animals *Dinosauria*, from the Greek words meaning "terrible lizard."

Owen became a celebrity in England. In 1851 he oversaw the construction of a dinosaur exhibit at the Crystal Palace in London. Thousands of visitors came to see life-sized models of Owen's dinosaurs.

Edward Drinker Cope
(1840–1897)

The rivalry between these two American paleontologists resulted in significant progress in the science of paleontology.

Othniel Charles Marsh
(1831–1899)

The Bone Wars

Othniel Charles Marsh and Edward Cope were friends who occasionally collected fossils together. In fact, they were such good friends that each named a species of dinosaur they found after the other. However, professional jealously ended their friendship. Their arguments became known as "the bone wars." Even the popular press reported on the disagreements between these two scientists.

Marsh was the director of the Peabody Museum of Natural History at Yale University. Cope was with the Academy of Natural Sciences in Philadelphia. Each man had his own approach to paleontology. Cope worked in the field with his teams. Marsh supervised his field researchers from his post at the museum, studying—and taking credit for—their discoveries.

These two paleontologists were not the first or the last scientists to disagree about the results of a study on dinosaurs. Often, however, the attempt to resolve a controversy produces new knowledge.

Dinosaur tracks in the Mojave Desert

Warm-blooded or cold-blooded?

Warm-blooded animals create their own body heat and maintain a constant body temperature. Their heart rate is higher than that of cold-blooded animals. The body temperature of cold-blooded animals is determined by their environment. Cold-blooded animals become **sluggish** when the temperature is too cold.

Scientists are conducting experiments to find out which category dinosaurs fall into. They are comparing thin slices of fossilized dinosaur bones with those of non-extinct animals under microscopes.

Scientists are also looking at predator-to-**prey** ratios to solve this question. Warm-blooded carnivores need to live in an environment where plenty of prey is present. Scientists hope to find out if dinosaurs were warm-blooded or cold-blooded by how much prey there was at the time they lived.

A model of the carnivore *Gigantosaurus*

Emu

Are birds related to dinosaurs?

This question has been explored since the 1800s, when Sir Richard Owen first studied it. Today some paleontologists think that birds are simply evolved forms of small dinosaurs.

Scientists have come to this conclusion by comparing the anatomy of birds to that of dinosaurs. They have found many similarities in the structures of their body parts. The feathers of birds may be seen as a version of dinosaur scales. This theory has become so well accepted that emu footprints have been studied in order to learn more about dinosaur tracks.

What happened to the dinosaurs?

There are plenty of theories about what happened to the dinosaurs. Paleontologists continue to study the fossil record and have come up with popular theories.

Some Theories

- A giant volcanic eruption sent a large cloud into the atmosphere that kept out sunlight. Plants died, so dinosaurs could not get the food they needed and starved to death.
- Mammals ate the eggs from the dinosaurs' nests or ate the dinosaurs themselves.
- An asteroid hit Earth and stirred up such a cloud of dust that the climate changed, freezing the dinosaurs.
- The dinosaurs developed severe allergic reactions to the increasing number of flowering plants (though most scientists think this theory is pretty unlikely).

A fossil of the flying
dinosaur, *Pterodactylus*

Practicing Paleontology

Practicing paleontology requires years of study in zoology, biology, botany, and geology. There are many amateur paleontologists who dig for fun and make exciting fossil finds too. Some work in their own backyards, and some join digs that are led by professionals.

Today many expeditions take place in **volcanic** environments. Volcanic ash contains fossils that can be dated by a method called radiometrics. This measures the radioactivity level left in the remains. The less radioactive material left in the fossil, the older it is. (The level of radioactivity is not **poisonous** to humans.)

Paleontologists carry picks and shovels to do serious digging. They also carry small tools for delicate work with **fragile specimens**. The work can be difficult. It takes experience to recognize a fossil. The discovery is not the end of the work either. Fossils must be prepared for study in a way that will preserve them. Everything a paleontologist discovers is a piece of evidence that may help to answer questions about ancient life forms.

A fossilized part of the lower jaw from a prehistoric big cat

Is there a future for paleontology?

Paleontologists still do not know all there is to know about prehistoric life and dinosaurs. There are many unanswered questions.

Since paleontologists are scientists, they know that each new piece of information may mean rethinking their theories about dinosaurs. Remember that the bone Robert Plot thought might have come from a giant human was later identified as part of a *Megalosaurus*.

Paleontologist James Hagadorn climbs a rocky hill in Death Valley, searching for rocks that may contain traces of prehistoric animal life.

There are many more fossils still to be found. Since Earth is constantly shifting, fossils that have been buried can appear after an earthquake, when ground is broken for a new highway, or simply after erosion over time.

So head out to your backyard, the beach, or the park. Keep your eyes open. Examine all the rocks and the shells that you find. If you decide to dig, make sure you have permission. Remember that Mary Anning was your age when she made her first contribution to paleontology!

Glossary

fragile *adj.* easily broken, damaged, or destroyed; delicate; frail.

poisonous *adj.* containing a dangerous substance; very harmful to life and health.

prey *n.* animal or animals hunted and killed for food by another animal.

sluggish *adj.* slow-moving; not active; lacking energy or vigor.

specimens *n.* samples.

treacherous *adj.* having a false appearance of strength, security, etc.

volcanic *adj.* of or caused by a volcano; about volcanoes.